BETTER BUSINESS COMMUNICATION

A *QUICK* GUIDE TO

I0485875

BETTER

PRESENTATIONS

HEATHER WRIGHT

Heather Wright
hwrightwriter@gmail.com

Book Layout ©2013 BookDesignTemplates.com

Image courtesy of David Castillo Dominici at FreeDigitalPhotos. Full Portfolio available at
http://www.freedigitalphotos.net/images/view_photog.php?photogi
d=3062

Better Business Communication
A Quick Guide to Better Presentations/ Heather Wright. —1st ed.

ISBN 1517556945

Get the entire Better Business Communication series in **ONE, COST-SAVING VOLUME**! The complete contents of

- *A Quick Guide to Writing Better Email*
- *A Quick Guide to Better Writing & Grammar*
- *A Quick Guide to Better Presentations,* and
- *A Quick Guide to Better Telephone Skills* are all **here**:

Check your online bookstore for more details

Contents

Introduction.. 1

Tip 1: Planning.. 3

    IN SHORT.. 5

Tip 2: Thinking of the Audience 7

    IN SHORT.. 8

Tip 3: Biting the Bullets... 11

    IN SHORT.. 12

Tip 4: Fonts & Color... 13

    IN SHORT.. 17

Tip 5: Sound & Action.. 19

    IN SHORT.. 20

Tip 6: The Handout 21

    IN SHORT.. 22

Tip 7: Charts & Tables.. 23

    IN SHORT.. 24

Tip 8: The Singer not the Song 25

    IN SHORT.. 29

Tip 9: Be Prepared 31

Step 10: Proofread – Errors look worse in 30 font

.... 35

Last Words 37

Introduction

This book is **your quick guide to better presentations**. In ten short chapters, you'll have the strategies you need to create viewer-friendly presentations and to develop the speaking skills you need to mark you as a professional.

Like every other form of business communication, **presentations have two purposes:**

    1. to make your company look good.

    2. to make you look good.

This book will refer to PowerPoint® presentations but you can extrapolate the guidelines to any presentation format you choose. A format that adds more movement to your presentation or has backgrounds that are more interesting isn't necessarily more accessible or more appreciated by your audience.

If you're going to apply the KISS principle (*Keep It Short and Simple*) to any form of business communication, your presentation is the one to pick. The strategies that follow will help you make a good impression and avoid boring your audience, and give you a pattern to follow that will make you a sought after presenter.

Other books currently being released in this Better Business Communication series cover the topics of writing better emails, and telephone skills. Look for further volumes in the series later this year covering common grammar/writing problems and writing persuasively.

CHAPTER 1

Tip 1: Planning

To start planning your presentation, here are some questions you should ask:

- What's the purpose of my presentation? To explain, sell, lead a discussion, teach a concept?
- Who is my audience? How much does my audience know about the subject of my presentation already? (We'll look more closely at the topic of audience in Chapter 2.)
- How much time have I been allotted?
- What setting will I be in? Board room with senior management? Auditorium with 300 people? Meeting room with ten or twenty people? Will they be eating? Are they expected to take notes?

The purpose of your presentation affects several things.

If you're explaining or describing a new product or a change in company policy, you'll need to make sure that your audience goes home with written material to refer to later. If the topic is complex, your job is not to make it more so. Think about how you can simplify the material into as few slides as possible to give the audience an over view, and allow them the time to ask questions or talk to you later about details they have discovered in the written material.

If the content could be upsetting to your audience (bad news regarding layoffs or a decrease in company benefits) most of your time should be spent talking to the people in the room and showing empathy rather than flashing a series of slides at them. For them, the information you are passing on will change their lives. Being present as a person is more important than the history of the company's slide to insolvency.

If you are there to lead a discussion or a brainstorming session, your slides should do no more than provide talking points.

If you are teaching a concept, make sure that your slides contain more than just bullet points, which your audience will read before you have addressed each one and then doze off to wait for the next one. Make sure that you find ways in the teaching time to get the audience involved. Break them into groups for short discussions or for hands-on trials of the points you are teaching. Nothing teaches better than hands-on learning.

With regard to the time you have allotted to you, please **ignore the old standby of one slide per minute.** You've sat through enough of these presentations yourself to know that it's a recipe for boredom, information overload, and surreptitious viewing of smartphones as an escape mechanism. Your job is to inform and entertain, where possible, but never to bore. We'll talk about how to work around this rule in Chapter 3.

Your setting influences the appearance of your slides, too. If you are addressing an auditorium full of people, bullet points are lost on the back row. Unless the hall is completely dark, the chance of people being able to read your material is slim.

Look for visuals that summarize or highlight your points. Your slides serve more to emphasize what you are saying rather than contain everything you are saying. If you have a group of people in a smaller room or around a board table, make sure that your slides work with the lights on in the room and that you allow time for discussion and audience involvement to ensure engagement.

IN SHORT

- Plan your presentation based on its purpose.

- Ignore the 1 slide/minute rule.
- Consider setting when designing the content of your slides.

CHAPTER 2

Tip 2: Thinking of the Audience

Consider who your audience is and **how much they know already.** If the information you are presenting is new to them, more background may be required.

Think about the age of your audience. Senior management may not appreciate your LOL references or what you might think are humorous comparisons to current pop musicians.

How many other presentations has your audience already sat through before yours? If your presentation is part of a series at an information day or conference, you need to find a way for your material and your presentation to stand out. You have competition for your audience's attention. As soon as the screen lights up, they're inwardly (or maybe not) rolling their eyes at yet another sixty PowerPoint® slides. What can you do that is different?

How early did they get up to drive to your presentation? Coffee can't solve everything, and since, at conferences, coffee is usually served with sugary treats, expect a sugar slump about 30 minutes into your presentation. What can you schedule at that time to keep your audience awake? Can you work in an activity where they have to get up and move or talk to a neighbor or gather in a group or solve a puzzle or … you get the idea.

Does your audience have to be there? Has management told them that they have to attend? If they are there because they have to be there, you might have a little hostility to overcome. They are likely leaving a desk-load of work behind, knowing that emails are pinging in all the time you are speaking that they will have to catch up on later

Be genuine in your appreciation of their attendance. Tell them that you value their time and prove it by ending a little early, or using a show of hands to skip a certain point if they already know it or have experience with it. Showing that you respect what they know is always a plus. Thank them sincerely when you are finished and give them the opportunity to reach you later with questions that they just can't stay and ask right now.

IN SHORT

- Consider your audience: how much they know, age, how many other presentations they will be attending, timing of your presentation

- Look for an activity about 30 minutes in to over come the meal/coffee break/sugar slump. Get them in groups, find a reason for them to move, challenge them to solve a puzzle, or throw out some trivia questions.
- Show that you appreciate their being there and that you value their time.

CHAPTER 3

Tip 3: Biting the Bullets

Your slides should never be your script.

I really mean it.

Every word you say should not be written on your slides—for a couple of reasons.

First, your audience reads faster than you speak. They will choose to read first and then simply wait for you to catch up and turn to the next slide. If you wanted them to sit and read, you could have printed out the presentation and handed it to them.

For example, if you are going to talk about three ways to improve your website, don't list all three ways and the explanations for each on your slide. **Use one-word hooks, or, even better, a visual.**

Using the example above, let's say that one way to improve a website is to have an interesting *About* page and that a successful *About* page has three components: a photo, a statement of purpose (why you felt it necessary to create the website), and some personal information that makes you interesting to the reader.

Instead of listing those three elements, why not have three visuals on your slide that you can talk about: a photograph frame, a big question mark, and a diary. Your visual learners will love you because they will be able to attach what you say to each of the symbols you've put on the screen. Aural learners will like it, too, because you're only asking them to listen rather than write, read, and listen at the same time. Your other learners will write the words down instead of the pictures anyway, and all will be good.

After you've explained the three necessary elements for a successful *About* page, **back up your theory with examples**. Use views of successful *About* pages or provide your audience with a list of links that they can check on their own later.

You are supposed to be the expert. They came to listen to you. Use the slides to keep their attention on you. This isn't a webinar. You are actually there--in 3D--and your audience wants to connect with you.

IN SHORT

- Your slides should never be your script.
- Use visuals instead of bullet points.
- Use examples.
- Remember, that they came to see and hear you.

CHAPTER 4

Tip 4: Fonts & Color

Here's how to apply the KISS principle to this component of your slides.

1. Use sans serif fonts.

They're easier to read from a distance or on a screen. The font for this book is Times New Roman, but on your e-reader you can choose whatever font is easier for you read. For presentations stick to something clean such as Arial or Calibri. You can see that the spacing and size are quite different for the two of them even though they are both font size 12.

2. Size matters.

The larger the font, the easier the slides are to read. Slides filled with lines of small dense text are an immediate turn off for your audience. Seriously, they won't even bother trying to read them. Keep the font large and simple, and **don't use FULL CAPS**, as they are hard to read at a distance, too.

PowerPoint® offers a large variety of design templates for you to use, but not all of them are going to be easy on your audience's eyes. Extra options, like VisualBee® have even more to choose from. As a rule, **avoid dark backgrounds** and avoid backgrounds that incorporate monochrome patterns.

Always try out your slides in a darkened room ahead of your presentation. Also, check them out in a lit room, too. On the day of the presentation, you might not be able to turn the lights down to the level you want in your presentation room. You might as well be prepared.

4. Colors

If you need to incorporate your company's colors, you can probably find the combination you need under the colors' drop down and use those colors in the borders of your slides only.

For example, if orange, black and white are your company colours, never use the orange for any words on the slides. It's not a good colour at a distance. But the color can be included in a banner across the bottom or along the slide, where you can also add a small version of your company logo.

Bright red or bright blue words on a black background can actually flare and look like they are moving when they are viewed on a screen. Very unnerving, especially if you haven't had that first—or second--cup of coffee. Remember that just because it looks good on your laptop screen, doesn't mean that it will look equally as good for your audience.

Good old black print on a white background is really just fine. Remember the slides aren't what are on show here; it's you and your message. What do you really want your audience to remember at the end of the day? If you make it easy for your audience to access the content, you are doing your job.

5. Italics or Not—Not!

For clean readable text, **avoid slanted fonts or the ones that look like handwriting**. There are lots of other ways to emphasize your text with bolding or highlighting.

Consider that, if you want certain words or phrases to stand out from all the other words, the other words might not have to be there in the first place.

For example, if the information on your slide looks like this—

THINGS TO DO BEFORE WRITING AN ESSAY

First, you need to **brainstorm ideas.**
Second, you need to **choose a topic** and **ask questions** about it.
Third, you need to go online or to the library to **find research resources**.
Fourth, you need to **draft an outline**.

it should probably look like this—

BEFORE WRITING AN ESSAY

1. Brainstorm ideas
2. Narrow the topic
3. Ask questions
4. Find research resources
5. Draft an outline.

While you are speaking, you can fill in the details about how to do all the items from 1 to 5. You can link the list items to examples, or get the audience involved by giving them a topic and asking them to give you their techniques for brainstorming, choosing a topic, etc.

IN SHORT

- Use sans serif fonts.
- Size matters.
- Keep the background clean.
- Colors are important
- No italics

CHAPTER 5

Tip 5: Sound & Action

You can **use both for emphasis, *once in a while,* BUT *not on every slide, please*.** When I first introduce PowerPoint® to my classes, the first thing I let them do is play with all the sound and animation tricks. The final results are lots of fun to watch and listen to, but a serious business presentation they are not.

Having your talking points appear on your slide as you make them or after you've made them for emphasis, works fine as a technique, but forget having them slide in and do a little dance every time, or shake, or swoop in with a big swishing noise. They're words not acrobats, and your audience will get tired of the tricks very quickly.

IN SHORT

- Use sound and action rarely.
- Have talking points appear after you've made the point. Treat them as end punctuation to what you are talking about.

CHAPTER 6

Tip 6: The Handout

Handouts are easy. PowerPoint provides a template for handouts of various configurations under the print function.

Not everyone takes notes the same way. The standard PowerPoint® handout lists three slides down the left side of the page and on the right are three groups of blank lines to use for writing notes. That style of note-taking appeals to many people, but there are others who need a little more space.

Take the same miniatures of your slides and centre them on the page with lots of empty white space around them. People like me are more spatial note takers. We like to draw arrows and write on the diagonal, circle things and create a final product that looks like a real mess to the linear note takers, but makes perfect sense to us.

Actually, we do the same thing even if you offer us lines to write on, but we appreciate the option.

It doesn't hurt to have a version of the handout that is in a larger font, perhaps only two slides to a page.

Not everyone has vision that switches well from looking at your slide to looking at the page. The larger print on the page will be more easily accessible to those who have some vision challenges in a dimly lit room.

Don't forget to **offer a follow up email** to those who are interested, so that any live links in your PowerPoint® can be available to them along with links to any other background information that might interest your audience. It's a great way to collect email addresses for your mailing list, and develop a ready audience for your next presentation.

IN SHORT

- Use the PowerPoint® handout template for linear thinkers.
- Create a handout for the spatial types.
- Create a handout in larger font for poorly lit rooms and attendees with vision challenges.
- Consider offering an email option

CHAPTER 7

Tip 7: Charts & Tables

Charts and tables can be a presenter's worst nightmare. First, you need to make the image large enough to be seen at the back of the room. If you are using a screen shot for your chart, how clear is it? Does enlarging make everything a bit out of focus? On the handout, will the image be too small to make any sense, especially if it's only printed in black and white?

If you want to discuss a particular, detailed image, print it in colour on paper and hand it out, so that it's large enough for people to read and refer to as you talk about the one you have projected on the screen.

Avoid overlaying data in various colours to show changes over time. It looks nice on your computer screen, but to an audience it can be confusing. Consider using handouts for this information, too.

I can't even think of this topic without immediately picturing the following video. If you do nothing else in this book, watch Don McMillan's hilarious *Life After Death By Powerpoint*:
https://www.youtube.com/watch?v=MjcO2ExtHso

There's a longer version available on YouTube as well. Enjoy.

IN SHORT

- Consider distributing a colour hard copy.
- Avoid overlaying a lot of data.
- **Watch the video**.

CHAPTER 8

Tip 8: The Singer not the Song

After the Starship Enterprise's course was locked in, Captain Jean Luc Picard's instructions consisted of one word, **engage**. That's your job—to engage your audience. Here are some tips to make sure that you do just that.

Face Front

The audience wants to see your face. Turning your back on them to read the content of your slide sends the wrong message. It says that you lack confidence, and that you didn't prepare well enough to know what you are supposed to say without reading it from the screen. That's not to say that you have to have everything memorized, but the notes you speak from should be in your hand or on the podium, not on the screen.

Eye contact

This can be hard to do, but it's easy to fake. If you are in a large room, you can simply look at the tops of people's heads. The people you are looking at will assume you are looking at the person behind them and the ones behind will think you are looking at the person in front of them. The rest of the audience will think, "What great eye contact!" Well, maybe not, but they will see you as confident enough to connect with an audience in stead of looking up into space or staring at the exit sign on the back wall.

Your Voice

If I suggest that you tape yourself as you practise your presentation, you will tell me that you hate your voice on tape. Me, too. In fact, we all do. The voice we hear is from the inside of our head, not the voice others hear on the outside. I, frankly, think I sound like Minnie Mouse, but that's another story.

The backbone of good speaking is good breathing. Every day you should practise breathing from your diaphragm. A voice that is fully supported sounds like it's in control and calm. If you are only breathing from the top half of your lungs, you will run out of breath a lot and sound as if you are anxious or nervous. When you listen to your voice, also listen for the breathing.

If you are wearing a mic for your presentation, it will pick up everything. Listen to some television commentators. Sometimes the mics pick up every inhale, and the commentators sound as if they are gasping for air. (Some interviewers on the Golf Channel come to mind, and it's also common among many guests on Sunday morning political interview shows.) Listen for that sound when you are speaking. Slow down and breathe quietly to avoid that gasp noise after every sentence.

Even if you don't like the *sound* of your voice, there are things that you need to pay attention to that will improve your chances of getting your message across.

Pace

If you rush, people will miss what you are saying. If they miss the content too often, they'll turn off entirely. When you try to slow down, you may think you are speaking glacially slowly. It really isn't the case. Making sure that each word is clear can take a little practice, but it's worth it. If you are using vocabulary that is new to your audience, make sure that you take your time to pronounce it clearly and that it turns up on the screen or on your handout, so that people don't get distracted trying to figure out what you are saying.

Pitch

If you think that your voice sounds too high, you may be right. Try pitching it a little lower. Lower voices convey more authority than high ones, and concentrating on lowering the tone of your voice a bit will also help you slow down. When you listen to your voice, also make sure that you have variety in your pitch and your volume. If everything you say stays all on the same note, the monotonous sound will be a sleeper for your audience.

Rise and Fail

If you want your audience to have confidence in you, don't sound as if every statement you make is a question. Many people have a tendency to raise their voices at the end of every sentence. They sound as if they are always asking a question. They also sound insecure and uncertain. Watch for this one, as it can undermine the confidence you want people to have in you and your message.

For a few more tips, here's a link to a great article by Gina Barnett, an experienced TED talk speaker coach: http://blog.ted.com/a-ted-speaker-coach-shares-11-tips-for-right-before-you-go-on-stage/

IN SHORT

- Face your audience
- Make eye contact
- Breathe from your diaphragm
- Speak slowly and clearly
- Pitch your voice lower for credibility
- Vary the pitch of your voice for emphasis
- Stop making every statement sound like a question

CHAPTER 9

Tip 9: Be Prepared

Stuff happens. Power cables break down. Projector bulbs burn out and there isn't a replacement. The venue's WiFi is unreliable or simply disappears. You can't get the darkness level you want in the room for your presentation, and now the room is so bright that people can't see the slides or so dark that they can't see to write notes.

Whatever you do, **don't spend a lot of time apologizing** for this. Everyone has been in situations where things have happened that are beyond his or her control. Today is your turn. Make a joke. Keep it light. Stay calm. There should be a hitchhiker's guide to presentations that also says in nice friendly letters, *Don't Panic.* Remember your audience is on your side. They want to learn what you are going to tell them. They want you to be a success, so they will meet you more than half way when things go wrong.

Here are some things you might consider as back up:

- If the room is too dark, see if you can open a door or two, preferably near the back of the room. Even a little light can make a big difference to people's comfort level. Room lights are often connected in banks, so play with them, always lighting the back of the room first, so that the slides are visible.
- If you can open a door that shines light on you but isn't too bright to wash out your images, then go for that, too. A poorly lit room means that your face might not be very visible. This means that your voice needs to be louder and clearer. (People hear better when they can see your face.) If people are seated around tables, walk the room a bit as you talk. You should have a hand remote that will control the slides from anywhere.
- Always have an easel, paper and markers on hand. Sometimes venues will provide these for you, but if they don't, it might be worth investing in them for yourself. If for some reason, you can't project your slides or they are barely visible because of a bright room, use the paper to write down your keywords or slide titles as you talk. The movement and writing gives people something to watch.
- If there are too many people for the expense of printing the typical PowerPoint® slide handout, which might be two or three pages,

consider making up a page that has just your slide topics listed. The audience can scribble on that while you speak. Have this prepared ahead of time. If you need it because of equipment breakdowns, your venue should be able to make copies for you quickly.

- Bring your own water. If you like your water cold, bring it in a cooler and consider using an insulated cup or put the water bottle in one of those sleeves that you put on beer and pop tins in the summer. You don't want to have to worry about your hands or anything else getting dripped on from the condensation.

- If the WiFi isn't working, don't apologize. It's not your fault. This is a good time to offer to collect email addresses, so you can send along the links later. Or send your audience members to your website where you will set up a link to your slides and the live links they need. Actually, you should probably have this set up before the presentation.

CHAPTER 10

Step 10: Proofread – Errors look worse in 30 font

Proofread your slides. If you think it's embarrassing to find a typo in an email to a coworker after you've hit send, imagine what a mistake looks like in 30 font to a group of people whose trust or business you are working to keep or earn.

Some proofreading tips:

- If possible, put the project away for a few days before you proofread. You're less likely to catch errors if the material is fresh in your brain because you'll be seeing what you think you wrote, not what you actually wrote.
- Print out your slides. Words look different on the page than they do on a screen. You can spot errors more easily.
- Read your slides in reverse order. Start at your last slide and work back to the beginning. In fact read your individual slides from the bottom up. Our brains are very good at

putting words where we expect them to be when they aren't really there at all.

- Use your finger to follow under the words as you are reading. This helps you slow down and actually look at the words.
- If you are using anyone's name or title of his or her book or company name or work title, double check that these are absolutely correct. Even the name Smith can be spelled more than one way.
- Let someone else have a look at it. Sometimes a fresh pair of eyes will see things that you don't.

Last Words

There is no magic bullet for success in your career, but you can bet that making a good impression through your communication skills won't hurt and may just set you above the rest.

Good luck with meeting your business goals. One of my goals is to sell more books. If you found this guide of value, please stop by your online bookseller and leave a review. I appreciate your time and your honest comments.

This book is not carved in stone either. If there are other issues about the topic that you think I should address, please drop me a line, and I can always add it to the next edition.

hwrightwrighter@gmail.com

ABOUT THE AUTHOR

Heather Wright is a freelance writer and part-time college instructor teaching business communications. Heather worked for many years in companies, both local and global in scope, and now runs her own freelance writing business. Through these experiences, she has developed her own communications skill set that she now shares in her Better Business Communications books and with her students, in the classroom, as well as, in the workplace.